1 2 3

Skills Workbook

This workbook belongs to

Use pencils, crayons, and stickers to complete the activities in this book. When there is a sticker missing, you will see this pattern:

one

Color the **1**.
Then sticker and count **1 sun**.

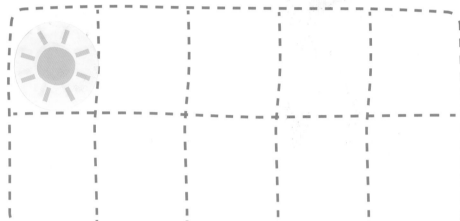

Trace the **1**'s.

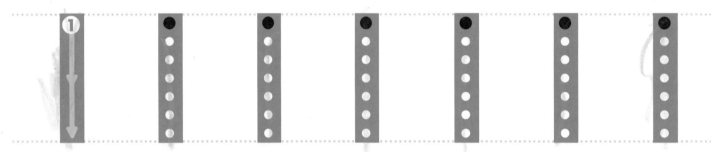

Trace the dotted line to find **1 bee**.

2

two

Color the **2**.
Then sticker and count **2 strawberries**.

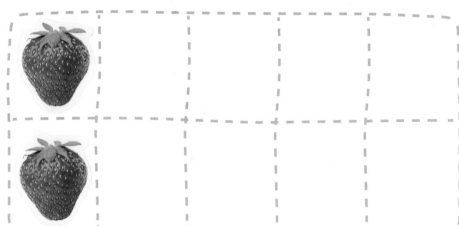

Color the dinosaur to make **2 dinosaurs**.

Trace the **2**'s.

three

Color the **3**.
Then sticker and count **3 cookies**.

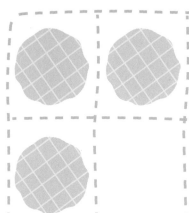

Trace the **3**'s.

Circle the plate with **3 cupcakes**.

four

Color the **4**.
Then sticker and count **4 flowers**.

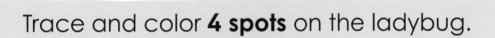

Trace and color **4 spots** on the ladybug.

Trace the **4**'s.

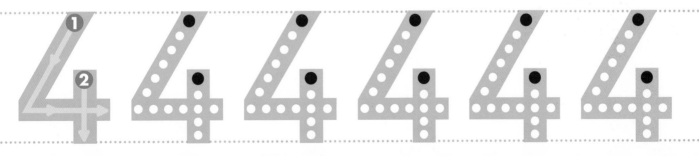

five

Color the **5**.
Then sticker, color, and count **5 faces**.

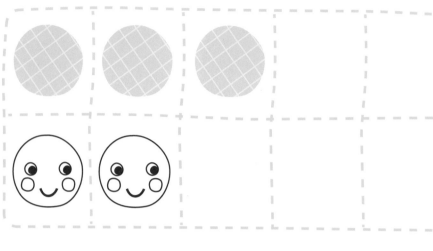

Trace the **5**'s.

5 5 5 5 5 5 5

Color **5 bananas** for the chimp.

six

Color the **6**.
Then sticker, color, and count **6 crowns**.

Trace **6 candy hearts**.

Trace the **6**'s.

7
seven

Color the **7**.
Then sticker, color, and count **7 balls**.

Trace the **7**'s.

Check the box by the pond with **7 ducks**.

eight

Color the **8**.
Then sticker, color, and count **8 apples**.

Trace the numbers to count the octopus's legs.

Trace the **8**'s.

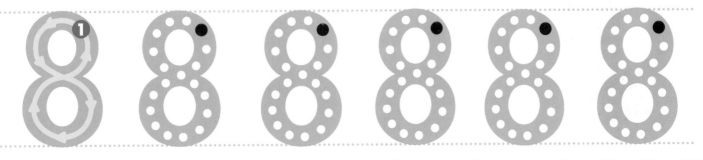

9
nine

Color the **9**.
Then sticker, color, and count **9 butterflies**

Trace the **9**'s.

9 9 9 9 9 9

Trace and color the sock to make **9 socks**.

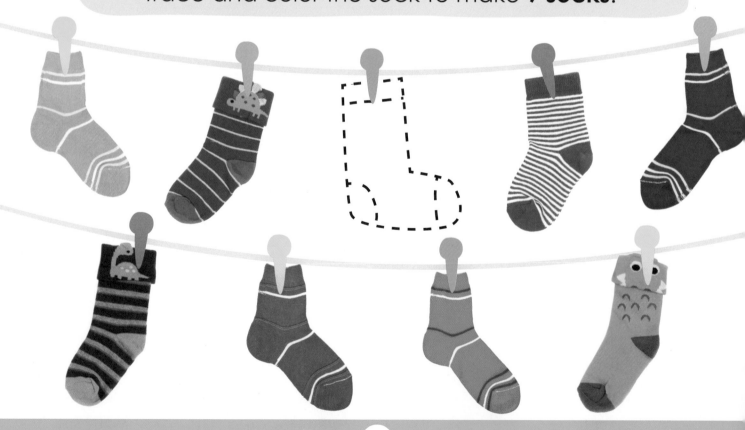

10
ten

Color the **10**.
Then sticker, color, and count **10 stars**.

Trace the numbers to count the fingers.

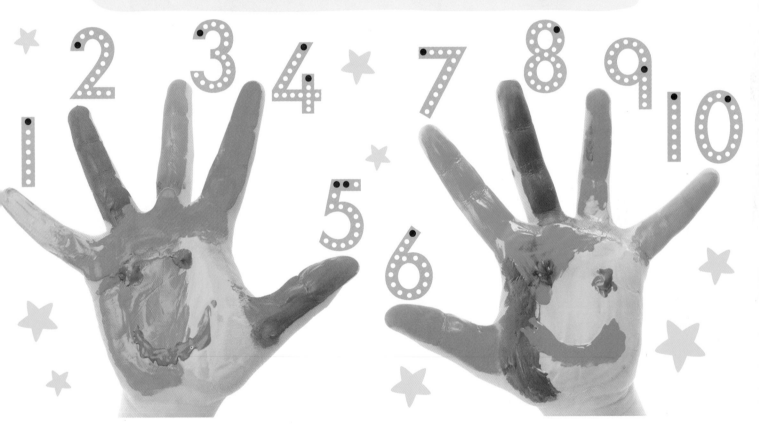

Trace the **10**'s.

Count and match

Trace the numbers, and draw lines to match the **numbers** to the **groups**.

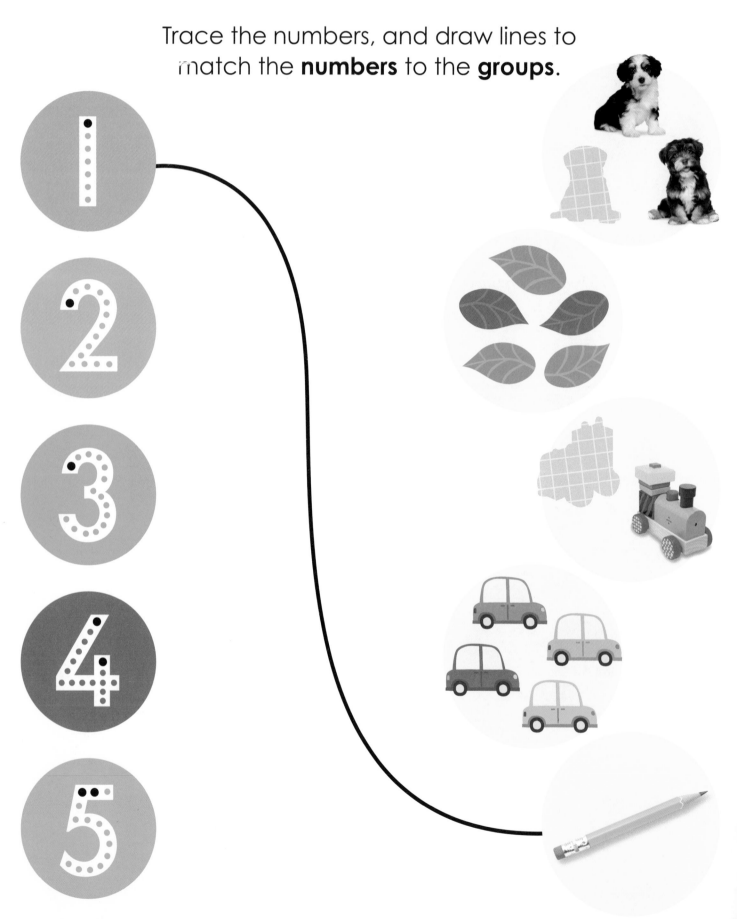

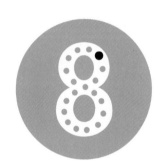

One more

Here are **3 butterflies**. Sticker **1** more to make **4 butterflies**.

Here are **5 Popsicles**. Sticker **1** more to make **6 Popsicles**.

Here are **7 balloons**. Sticker **1** more to make **8 balloons**.

One less

Here are **4 diggers**. Cross out **1** to make **3 diggers**.

Here are **6 crabs**. Cross out **1** to make **5 crabs**.

Here are **10 hats**. Cross out **1** to make **9 hats**.

Number art

Count the dots to figure out which **color**
to use in each part of the picture.

• = yellow   • • = red   • • • = blue

⁚⁚ = green   ⦂• = brown   ⁚⁚⁚ = orange

Maze fun

Help Little Bo Peep's sheep find the way home by following the numbers in the right order.

Finish

10

8   9

3   9

7

8

4   6

5

6

8

4   7

5

3   2

Start   1   2

Counting to 15

Count **11 flowers**. Color the last **1**.

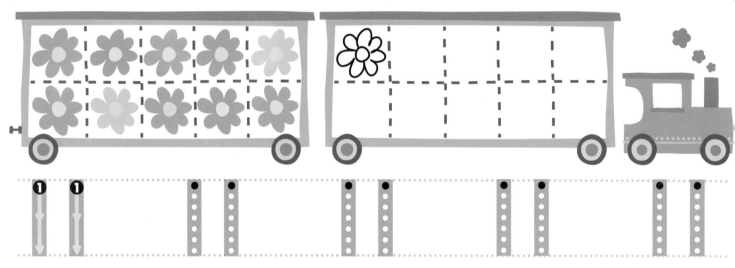

Count **12 trees**. Color the last **2**.

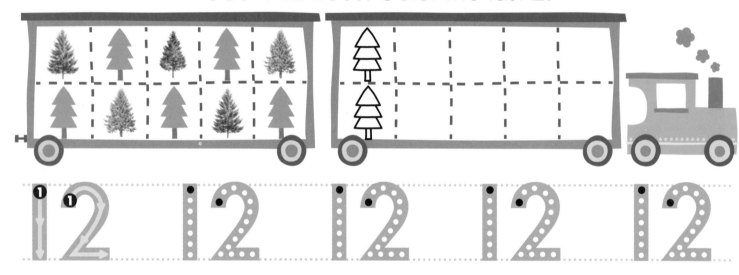

Count **13 birds**. Sticker the last **3**.

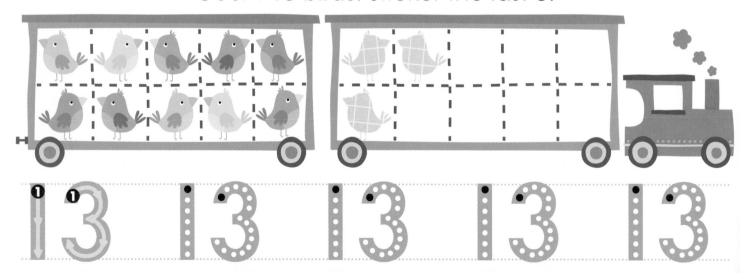

Count **14 stars**. Color the last **4**.

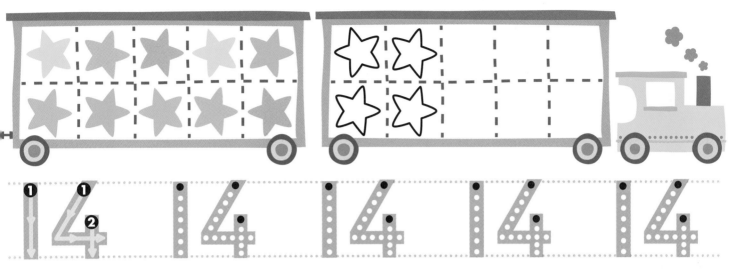

Count **15 balls**. Sticker the last **5**.

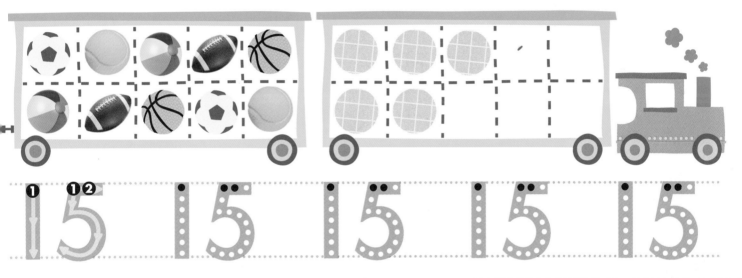

Trace the numbers from **11** to **15**.

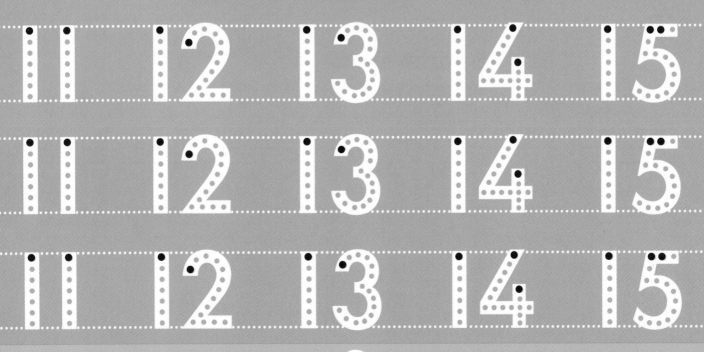

Counting to 20

Count **16 pumpkins**. Color the last **6**.

Count **17 lemons**. Color the last **7**.

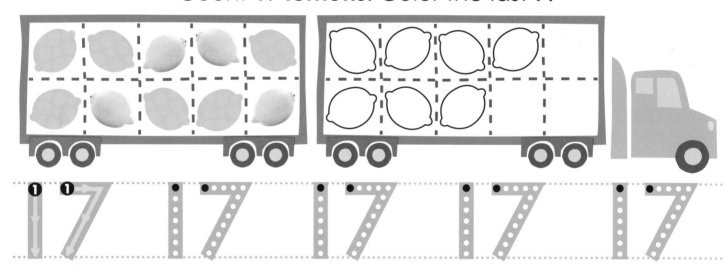

Count **18 frozen treats**. Sticker the last **8**.

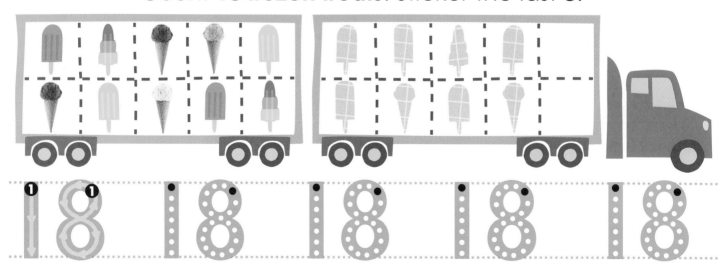

Count **19 cheese wedges**. Color the last **9**.

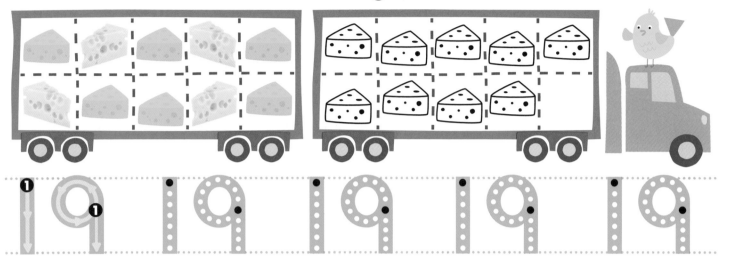

Count **20 cupcakes**. Sticker the last **10**.

Trace the numbers from **16** to **20**.

Dot-to-dot fun

Join the dots and finish coloring the picture.

Numbers to 20

Read and trace the numbers.

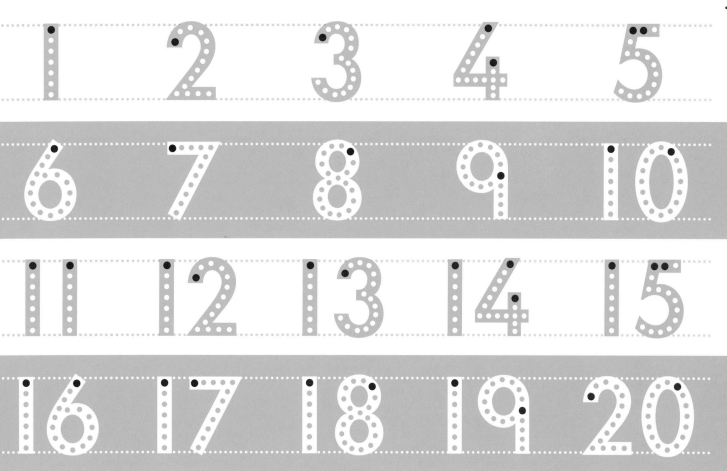

1 2 3 4 5

6 7 8 9 10

11 12 13 14 15

16 17 18 19 20

How many pieces of candy can you count?

Congratulations!

GOOD WORK AWARD!

Name: ....

has successfully completed the

123

Skills Workbook

Date: ....